Rhythm Wisdom

The Endangered Humans' Traveling Guide
—Vol. 1

Travis Jacobs

THRONE
PUBLISHING GROUP

Throne Publishing Group
220 S. Phillips Ave.
Sioux Falls, SD 57104
thronepg.com

Anita, you inspire me. I love you...

Years ago my addictions brought me a gift in the form of a message. The message was this: "We will kill you."

The gift of fighting for a life—yours or others—reveals interesting spaces on our journey; it opens our eyes to look at life in a new way, weighing what's really important and what's important to change. It can unclench hands and soften hearts. Bringing forth pieces of ourselves we had never seen before.

My friend Denny says to me often: "Son, when you find yourself with a problem, put pen to paper, and write yourself out of it." Sometimes the words came out as poems, or more like short stories. Other times they appeared like clenched prayers or partial pudding recipes. I chose to stitch the gifts shared with me by so many people and place the quilted patterns on these pages and call them Rhythm Wisdom. How do we realize the incredible value and potential each life holds, and how do we help it unfold? I hope these words will warm your path and encourage your journey along the way.

This is The Endangered Humans Traveling Guide.

Endangered Species

Endangered Species

Zebra Forest Treefrog
Yinnietharra Rock Dragon
Yellow-headed Temple Turtle
Wild Asian Buffalo
White-winged Wood Duck
Micronesian Imperial-pigeon
Toxopeus' Yellow Tiger
Western Lowland Gorilla
Volcano Rabbit
Karkloof Blue Butterfly
You

You are the last of your kind.

endangered species *noun – Any species of plant, animal, or other organism threatened with EXTINCTION. International and national agencies work to maintain lists of endangered species, to protect and preserve natural habitats, and to promote programs for recovery and reestablishment of these species.*

-Merriam Webster's online

At the writing of this book there are currently 10,796 animals on the endangered species list. I spent a day looking through the list and looking at their pictures. I looked up their habits, and read about their habitats, all beautiful, unique, and all with the possibility of being extinct. I think about the human being holding this book. Beautiful. Unique. And a 100% chance you are the last you.

There will never be another one of you. There will never be another one, with your physical, mental, or emotional makeup. There will never be another with your experiences, and events, or how you responded to them. There will never be another who lived in, endured, overcame, or changed the exact environments you have. If you were an animal and we put your name on a list, did a press release, and said:

"This is the last one." Groups of people would rally, funds would pour in, networks of people constructing a plan to help you survive and thrive. People would write articles about your importance, do news stories on your rarity, fly from around the globe just for you and your wellbeing.

This book is a press release to you, for you, saying we have to take care of you. Because you're worth it.

When we grasp the rarity and importance of our life, it changes how we look at it, how we treat it, and what we do with it. It makes us really evaluate the environments we put ourselves, the people we surround ourselves with, and it changes how we treat the lives of others.

The endangered list is printed again on the following page and there is a space for you to write your name.

Display it on your fridge.

Put it on your desk.

Hang it in your locker.

Read it in the morning; fold it up and put it in your pocket.

Or burn it and ask God to deliver the words directly to your heart.

Endangered Species

Zebra Forest Treefrog
Yinnietharra Rock Dragon
Yellow-headed Temple Turtle
Wild Asian Buffalo
White-winged Wood Duck
Micronesian Imperial-pigeon
Toxopeus' Yellow Tiger
Western Lowland Gorilla
Volcano Rabbit
Karkloof Blue Butterfly

Spencer Carter

You are the last of your kind.

RHYTHM WISDOM

8

Traveling Tip: Invest in yourself. With something as valuable as you, you must become willing to invest in you.

Every year I sit down with my daughter and give her some money I have saved just for this. I hand her the money and tell her I want to invest in her. Not because I expect a return on my investment, but because I see value and worth in her already. She is always worth investing in. So are you.

The only instructions for the money are: I want her to spend the money on something she loves, and she should try not to think about what other people, myself included, would think about what she's doing with the money.

We should do the same for ourselves, not because we are expecting a return and believe there will be value for our investment, but because we already see the value in us. It is also a great practice in not worrying what others think about what we are up to... and we should all be up to something that requires zero approval from people.

Traveling Transaction: How will you invest in you this year? Some people struggle with this because they haven't grasped the value of themselves yet. Remember, if you were the last polar bear, we'd be raising mass amounts of money to save you. Give yourself permission to invest in you.

Grim Reaper Grin on Me

You were sent here for a reason, and even if it takes you the rest of your life, you owe it to yourself to find out what that reason is.
        - Jonathan Kent to his son Clark, Superman (2013)

One afternoon I was sitting with my friend Don, who has lent me gallons of verbal wisdom and countless pages of priceless print in this life. After the recent passing of his wife, he shared with me the prayer he is holding onto for the rest of his life journey. It was: "God, don't let me die before I die."

A great place to start before embarking on any journey is checking the gauges, and while traveling through this universe a gauge we must check often is our pulse. Do I have one?

"If death found me today, would he find me living?" Am I spending the limited amount of time doing and pursuing the things that make me feel alive? Am I spending the limited amount of time I have with the people who make me feel alive? The day death finds me, what will he find?

One day while asking myself this question, I saw an image of the Grim Reaper in his common portrayal—death's boney finger pointing out from an oversized black shroud, and holding his haunting giant scythe in his other hand, looking for a victim to reap. This time I didn't see him as a dark demon with evil intent, looking to drag me down a shadowed corridor. He appeared more like a deliveryman, just doing his job and getting a bad rap for it. I saw a tired worker exhausted from all the disappointing times he found those he was sent to collect had already been dead long before he got there. I pictured instead how the Grim Reaper might look finding someone knowing they had lived fully. And in this case Death seemed more like a fanatic fan, cheering us on to live while we're alive and not die a second too early.

Grim Reaper Grin on Me

Grim Reaper grin on me.
When my watch will no longer wind.
When my heart's beat no longer keeps time.
Grim Reaper grin on me.
When my wells run dry.
For once a blank screen is all that's on my mind.
When a cold empty shell and warm soul alive is
    all you find.
Grim Reaper grin on me.
Grim Reaper grin on me before you shut my eyes,
    pay no attention to the number of years, see
    in their reflection how I lived, alive!
Grim Reaper look at the rings inside me,
    revealing a story like the timelines of a tree,
    see a life well lived.
Grim Reaper grin on me.
God, whatever happens, whenever it happens;
    don't let me be die before I die.
I wish to look down one last time at a grinning
    Grim Reaper enthusiastically nodding his
    head.
He knows what we know. At every intersection I
    chose to live alive instead of dead.

RHYTHM WISDOM

14

Traveling Tip: We know. We don't need a doctor to tell us if we have a pulse. We can choose for the remainder of this journey, resolve as a promise and gift to ourselves and those we love, to travel the trail we know our soul nudges us to go, so when we do "go," we go ALIVE!

"When death finds you, may it find you alive."

African Proverb

"I don't believe people are looking for the meaning of life as much as they are looking for the meaning of being alive."

-Joseph Campbell

PERMISSION SLIP

From this day forward I give myself permission to live my own life.

_____

Signature

_____

Date

Permission to Travel

Plenty of people rarely get the permission, chance, or the encouragement to live their life, change their life—to be themselves, to experience, to express and enjoy their journey.

When we are not given permission to be who we are, it makes perfect sense why we never feel like we have permission from this world or its people to pursue or do whatever we feel is best for us.

Worrying about what others think or expect from us can keep us in a string of unhealthy spaces with unhealthy people. It can keep us from traveling to some incredible experiences waiting for us in this universe.

Here is the secret to permission… you don't need it. No one holds your imaginary permission slip. But if we have been tricked into thinking someone does, or we unknowingly placed the permission slip in someone's hands for whatever reason, right here, right now you place the permission back where it belongs—in your possession.

This permission list is a start to do a lot of things people don't believe they have permission to do. You can use it; add to it or throw it away if you like, you don't need my permission to do whatever you choose with it.

A Lifetime Permission Slip

A lifetime permission slip to just be.
You have permission to do what you love.
To start chasing that dream.
To change what the dream looks like midstream.
To change the dream altogether.
To not know all the answers.
To not know any answers.
To know some answers.
To not know what you want.
To leave a job.
To buy a dog.
To take the dog back.
To make mistakes.
To fail.
To cry.
To feel how you feel.
To not know how to feel.
Permission to be happy.
You have permission to leave a relationship.
To start a relationship.
To do something embarrassing.
To spill something.
To break something.

You have permission to leave the house without
makeup on for as many days as you wish.
You have permission to weigh whatever it is you
weigh today.
You have permission to never weigh yourself
again.
You have permission to stop lying to yourself that
you'd magically feel better if something about
you looked another way.
You have permission to take care of yourself.
Touch yourself.
Tell someone they can never touch you again.
You have permission to get sober.
Stay sober.
To be really, really, really, angry.
To change.
To stay the same.
You have permission to have fun.
To accept an invitation.
To decline an invitation.
To end a conversation.
To avoid a conversation.
To avoid something or someone for the rest of
this journey.
To not take a phone call.
To not return a phone call.
To fart in public.
To try something new.
To not try something new.
To not apologize.
To stand up for yourself.
To like yourself.
To love yourself.
To love someone else.
To let someone love you.
To swear.

To make mistakes (I know this is on the list twice,
    you have permission to make more than one.)
You have permission to get up and walk out
    when someone is talking or acting in a way
    you don't feel comfortable being around.
Permission to remove yourself from situations.
Permission to remove people from your contact
    list.
To make things right.
To hang on.
To let go.
To fight.
To wanna give up.
To give up.
You have permission to forgive someone.
To forgive someone when we're ready.
You have permission to stop believing any and all
    negative BS about yourself.
You have permission to talk about whatever you
    feel it is you're not supposed to talk about.
To earn what you're worth.
To laugh till it hurts.
To play during the day.
To think what you think and believe what you
    believe.
Permission to stop trying to live up to
    expectations placed on you.
Permission to stop trying to come up with
    expectations for others.
To travel well and enjoy the journey.
You have permission to be you and never
    apologize for it.
You have permission to: _____
You have permission to: _____
You have permission to: _____
You have permission to: _____

RHYTHM WISDOM

22

Traveling Tip: A lot of anxiety and worry could be cut in half if we would just give ourselves permission to fail. The worry of trying to prevent failing, get things perfect, or not hurt others by living our own life has been the robber of peace for too many for far too long. Is there something you need to give yourself permission for today?

One of the best gifts we can give someone is the permission to be themselves without them ever feeling like they needed it from us in the first place. That is a beautiful relationship.

"I'm not in this world to live up to your expectations and you're not in this world to live up to mine."

-Bruce Lee

Bobbi Blisters Worn Wisdom

The "Choose your Own Adventure" style books are incredible. There are multiple outcomes, adventures, and endings in a single book. The reader is asked to choose what direction the hero of the story would take. Same is true for you. You are living a story. We have choices to make, but rarely weigh and sift the weight each road carries.

The Legend of Bobbi Blisters

Inked in honesty by rough, rugged hands of men, women, and desert trolls missing middle fingers and morals–who swore oaths on stacks of Bibles filled with blank pages. These are the somewhat true accounts of what they witnessed with keen eyes and clouded insights... This is the slightly massaged Legend of Bobbi Blisters.

Three days before turning fourteen Bobbi Blisters proved to be the fastest and most fearless gun in the west. Bobbi Blisters pumped Bobby Barrringer full of ten gauge buck shot two buttons below his top button, and directly beneath a tree, filled with four newborn baby blue jays in crowded sparrow's nest. They say one of those baby birds died from fright. The other three grew up hard-hearted, hard of hearing, never sung a song, and never left the nest.

Bobbi Blisters acquired a body count of over 15 by age18, including Bobby Two Toes of the Tetons, Bobby Burlap Saddles, and Bobbi East Coast.

With the undoing of Bobbi East Coast, Bobbi
Blisters became the fastest and most feared
gun in the west. And now the east as well.

The Legend of Bobbi Blisters grew like most
legends and pot-bellied pigs do: quickly and
slightly sideways.

Bobbi Blisters, fastest and most feared gun in the
east and west hopped a train going south, and
bumped into Bobby Memphis.

Bobby Memphis was known to carry a straight
razor in his crooked boots.

Bobby Memphis was not one for being bumped
into, and never one to apologize. So he made
this an instance to be settled by violence.

After a little cuss'n and a lot of cut'n, Bobby
Memphis ended Bobbi Blisters streak at the
ripe old age of 23.

Before the story hit the nearest town, Bobby
Memphis's ego-inflated head hit the
unforgiving ground.

Bobbi Bell Peppers had spent 2 years gunning
for Bobbi Blisters, had to settle for Bobby
Memphis. A less impressive story, but still
acquired the titles none the less

Bobby Bell Peppers was now known for pulling
the fastest gun in the west, east, and now
south. He was also known for growing the
biggest, brightest, bell peppers in the medium
sized mining town of Little Doubt.

Three weeks later his time and title had run out.
The flashy and dashing Bobby Peacock made
sure Bobbi Bell Peppers died with a purple
feather in his mouth.

Bobby Peacock was now the fastest, flashiest, and
most feared gun in the east, west, and south.
Having the grand personality he did, Bobby

Peacock assumed someone should make sure
they had heard of him in the Midwest. Bobby
Peacock settled on himself to be that someone
to spread the great, grand story of himself.
Bobby Peacock met Bobbi Vice Grips outside of
the Canton Cantina.
Bobbi Vice Grips had never heard the story
of the fastest flashiest, most feared gun in
the east, west, or south, but he had heard
of the man who invented the "British Man
Stopper" hollow points, and that ended Bobby
Peacocks story with an exclamation point!
Bobby Peacock's bright personality turned
grey. The titles he once carried floated to the
shoulders of another man.
Bobbi Vice Grips was a black smith, and to him
titles were of no interest, but that doesn't
matter if you choose to tangle with men
who busy themselves, making names for
themselves.
Bobbi Markers was Bobby Peacocks second
cousin never removed. Bobbi Markers traded
Bobbi Vice Grips two for two. Bobbi Vice
Grips found a shoulder and grazed a scalp.
Bobbi Markers found one in front and one in
back. Story has it the second shot came from
a little help.
Bobbi Markers enjoyed the fame for all of a
four-day ride to Colorado, were Bobby Two
Elks waited for him to pass by a barkless
berry tree. Bobbi Markers suffered from an
iron deficiency, and with what little he had
left, ran all out while he leaned up against that
barkless berry tree.
Bobby Two Elks killed Bobbi Markers in the
darkest hour of 1863.

This cold-blooded killing was filled with irony,
since markers weren't even invented 'til seven
years after 1903.

So much irony metaled in this affair, they say,
as late as 88 the berries themselves from the
bark less berry tree tasted a hint of iron.

And so it went on and on, round and round …

Bobbi Clockwerk, Bobby Tallgrass, Bobby
Johnny, Johnny Bobby, Bobby Bobbi, Bobby
Boilermakers, Bobbi Buttons, and Bobby 2
Left Boots. Then came Bobby 4 Jackets, Bobby
6 Caskets, and Bobby The III… It became
such a manic mess to try and track down the
trail of who held the elusive title from day to
day that they decided to end this once and for
all with a big Bobby Brawl. All the remaining
Bobby's met just west of southern North
Dakota, outside the "Not Everything is O.K.
Coral."

All the big and small player Bobbi's in the world
were there: Bobbi Leathers, Bobby Worthing,
Bobby the Lame, Bobby Two Bolts, and
Bobby The Insane (who they say had shown
symptoms of loose springs in the mental
machinery since he was sixteen). There was
Bobby Brass whose knuckles, bullets, belts,
and buckles were all made of clay. Bobbi
Southern Baptist, a Latin Lutheran minister
from Northern Lakes Minnesota, was there
for no other reason other than he was taking
a season off from God.

All the Bobbi's with a "Y", Bobby's with an "I", all
of them—even a Bobbi with no eyes.

They figured the best way to settle the rightful
owner of the title once and for all was to
make a circle…

On the count of one, everyone ready's
    themselves...
On the count of two every one aims...
On the count of three everyone fires...
Last man standing wins.
It was decided the drug store's co-owner Kyle
    Kelly would do the counting, since he had no
    skin in the game, or no name in the game for
    that matter.
One... They all readied
Two... They all aimed
Before Kyle could maneuver his lips to
    manipulate the syllable sounds of three,
    Bobby Two Elk's uncles, Bobbi Buffalo Skins,
    and Bobby Midnight Moon Winds both
    walked out into the center circle, only armed
    with clarity. They walked slowly like wisdom
    often does, and spoke about how this had all
    started years ago.
Bobbi Buffalo Skins explained: "One night Bobbi
    Blisters borrowed a shovel of Bobby Midnight
    Moon Winds, Bobbi dug all night and
    returned in the morning with the shovel and
    two handfuls of blisters.
At the time no one knew it, but Bobbi Blisters
    had spent the night burying the sins of the
    brutal Bobby Barringer, who had erased the
    lives of Bobbi Blister's parents the day before
    Bobbi Blister's fourteenth birthday.
Bobbi wasn't always a Bobbi, but all the bandits
    who rode with Barringer were–Bobby Two
    Toes of the Tetons, Bobby Burlap Saddles and
    Bobbi East Coast. The name Bobbi seemed a
    better fit for fitting in while fixin' to fix them.
    The blisters faded slowly, but the nickname
    stuck indefinitely, and as a constant calloused

reminder of the pain. Bobbi Blisters set out
for revenge, not for the fame of the name.

The title you are all searching for came from a
child's nickname trying to soothe and chase
away some pain, the way children often do, by
causing more pain.

Healthy adults have learned other ways to heal,
and set things right in themselves.

As Bobbi Buffaloskins and Bobby
Midnightmoonwinds started to gently walk
out of the circle.

Bobby Tallgrass asked: "So, what was Bobbi
Blister's name then, his real name?"

Bobbi Buffalo Skins replied: "Evelynn, her name
was Evelynn, little Evelynn Anderson."

All the Bobby's stood still, even the breeze took
a second to stand stunned. Dust was the only
thing that kept moving, tumbling a tumble
weed the size of a wagon wheel through the
circle, but no one seemed to notice.

They all thought about how everything had
gotten so out of hand, what little heart some
of them had left, pumped the low, hollow,
achy kind for a little girl who lost her parents,
and each Bobby took a second to reflect on
why they started this pursuit for themselves
in the first place.

Just then Bobby Hindsight, who was blind in one
eye yelled out:

"THREE!"...

Traveling Reflection: Often I have started headfirst down a path, chasing something or someone, sometimes for years, without ever asking myself: "Why am I choosing this for my life?" The good and the bad. Why do we pursue what we do, why do we pursue who we do? The sports we play, the hobbies we have, the career paths. The clothes we wear, the addictions we feed. Why did we choose them in the first place? What are my motives, and why do I seek what the actions and activities bring to me? Have I realized every path I pick and choose to travel has a price, and a payoff?

Traveling Tip: The next time you decide on a new diet, new haircut, new relationship, or accept the promotion ask, "Why am I really doing this, really?" Our motives and motivations can determine not only the success of what we're doing; it can also show us if we're setting ourselves up for a painful end to a journey.

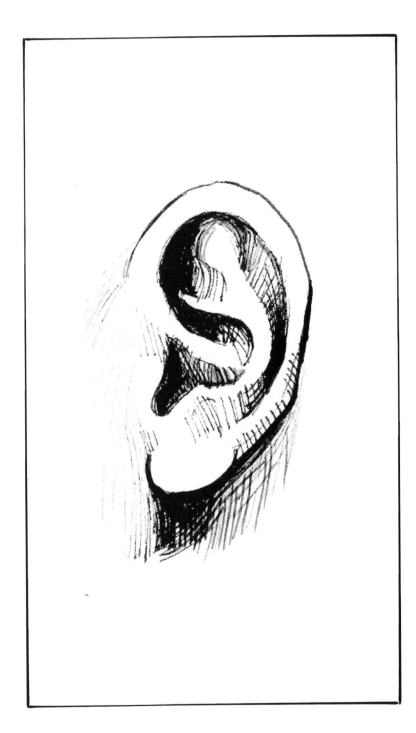

Come to Our Senses

I can't even count the number of times I've been in the room physically present, but mentally somewhere else. Someone is talking, and I might even be looking directly at them, but I don't hear a word they say.

I say prayers because I believe God listens to them; I believe people talk to each other because we believe people are listening to us.

More Valuable than Gold

Listen.
Listen like it's something you've never heard
    before.
Listen to the knock knock jokes you've heard a
    thousand times.
Listen to the jokes that aren't funny at all.
The details, as they rabbit-trail through a mapless
    labyrinth, and the rambling stories.
About the life-changing 15% off sale at the mall.
Listen to the exciting, the boring, and the
    mundane–listen to it all.
Whether you're in the mood, or could care less.
Listen to them.
Don't let your eardrums develop a numbness to
    the gift of them.
While people are here, listen like it's something
    you've never heard before, like there is gold
    dripping from every simple syllable, and you
    are a prospector collecting a treasure you
    have been digging your entire lifetime to find.
Collect all their words, and store the
    conversations in the mine of your heart.
Because.

When people are gone, hearing their voice one
last time is a wish we would all like granted.
And no matter how many lamps we rub, genies
we try to barter with, this wish will never be
granted.
So while they're here, try with every ounce in
you to never take their original one-of-a-kind
voice for granted again.
Their value is real and it outweighs gold or
anything else trying to steal our attention
from them.
Listen.
Listen to them.

Traveling Gift: The more we listen, the more we will hear.

Exercise the Eyes

If we would take the time to look people in the eyes, we would see more of their story than we ever thought possible.

Eyes

Eyes that carry joy.
Eyes that flirt.
Eyes that water from wind, and eyes that carry
    too much dirt.
Eyes of hardship.
Eyes that carry leadership.
Eyes that carry addiction.
Each addiction carries a different look.
Eyes that carry cancer, and eyes that love
    someone carrying cancer.
Eyes carrying an undiagnosed disease, and eyes
    carrying peace.
Eyes carrying airport luggage, and eyes hauling
    life luggage.
Eyes that carry the bulk of raising kids alone, or
    mostly on your own. A look of fulfillment
    clouded with abandonment, dashed with the
    extra love and extra hugs that had to land
    somewhere.
We've all seen these looks in the eyes of others,
    and others we've seen in the mirror.
Eyes cannot contain the deep, heavy pains some
    carry. It's not always kept out front. Look deep.

The pain can be placed towards the way, way, way
    back towards the end of the eyeball alleyway.
It was said eyes are the gateway to the soul.
It was said Lincoln's eyes were cut like deep
    caverns.
They say eyes stay open after you die because all
    your muscles relax.
I think it's because they want one last look.
Eyes are a neat soul check tool.
Can I see your eyes?
I need to see your soul, quick.
I need to reflect off yours, so I know I still have
    mine.

Traveling Tip: See how many times a day you can look people in the eye and really see them.

Traveling Gift: The more we look, the more we see.

AS SOON AS YOU TRUST YOURSELF YOU WILL KNOW HOW TO LIVE
JOHANN WOLFGANG VON GOETHE.

Exercise the Gut

Have you ever heard the story of the bomb-sniffing dog who didn't trust her instincts the first day on the job, and what happened the second day on the job? No, you haven't. There is no story about the dog's second day on the job. Some people call it a sixth sense; some people call it intuition, some people call it a gut feeling. Shoo this gift away, disregard it too often, and the voice or feeling grows softer, goes in the other room, but it never leaves us completely. Instincts are as much a part of us as any limb. Look down at a part of your body now: it's there and so are your instincts and intuition. Trust it.

Our instincts are a traveling gift. They will keep us out of danger, lead to better places and people we love.

The direction you're headed is imbedded in us like a GPS. Most travelers forget the compass, neglect its guidance, and we fail to realize we've always been equipped with all the tools necessary for the journey. After a counseling session with a man I can never repay, he said these words: "You know where you're going, and when you don't, you'll figure it out." I went back to my hotel and wrote this story.

Thank you, John.

This Compass

This compass was a gift.
At the creation train station that resembled a
    dark, gray, shaded version of Santa's "I-hope-
    this-works" shop.
There was a line intertwined and woven around
    with goblins, demons, and angels handing
    them down.
They sat atop along tabletop.
Giving gifts, curses, knowings, beliefs, faiths,
    doubts, fears, loves, likes, dislikes, tears, trials,
    tribulations, powers, and weaknesses.
Rummaging through a warehouse-sized junk
    drawer for a clue of what life had in store.
I was unsure at the time of what kind of creature
    stood before me.
"*Old Tattered*" peered down, over the top of her
    jet-black terminator-type sunglasses, like I
    was Sean Connor.
And she was thinking…
"Have you seen this boy?"
She wore a Sinead O'Connor shaved crew cut,
    jet-streamed blue eyes, and fluttering her
    Swiss cheese hole shaped wing (the one that

still remained fully intact).

Her cigarette dangled at an angle, out the corner of
her mouth holding a good fifteen-minute ash;
ready to drop atop my forehead at any minute.

If it fell, silence would be my only yell, as I still
had not received my voice.

I had no mouth to ask the many questions like
"Why is 'she' my angel?" "Is she an angel or
demon?" "Does it matter?" "Why does my
compass pass from her hand into mine?"

Is the smile she wears mischievous? Did she
bend up some of my compass springs when
no one was looking?

Or maybe she took some of the pieces out?

Who are all these people?

Where are we headed? Why do we need all these
things? Did I get too much faith? Do I need
more love, are you sure this is enough doubt?

I hear over the much-too-loud speaker: "All
aboard, last call for those holding tickets to
LIFE, climb aboard!"

I pick up my sack and heave it over my shoulder;
my shoulders will grow into it in the coming
years. What now seems like more stuff
than I could possibly ever use, there will be
days ahead where I'll wonder, "Is this stuff
enough?"

I look back at "*Old Tattered*" and realize the
smile she wears is not mischievous… it's
warm, loving, and promising of what is to
come. She sends me on my way with a "hang
in there" wink of what she knows is to come.

While on the train, I sifted through my duffle
bag and found a note attached to my compass.
It read: "The big guy forbids any notes of
instruction, but if He really cared about the

rule He would have made sure I hadn't put
this in here. This bag is yours and no one
else's; you will need everything in this bag. At
times people, places, and life's problems may
get you temporarily off track. At times people,
places, and problems will help steer you back.
At times people, places, and life's problems
will seem too big to handle, and appear as
if fate's chisel has set them in stone. In these
times, son:
Gently sit yourself down on the side of the road.
Take out your pack, and use your compass; climb
over, walk around, and dynamite just enough
space for yourself to crawl through.
Remember this above all things: Your compass is
never broken; it will never lead you off course.
Know no matter how high you have climbed,
or how far down you have gone, it will always
point you back to true North. The only way
it will start to feel broken and not working is
when it points you in the right direction and
you...
Just then, an open window from the back of the
train sucked the note out of my hands before I
could finish the rest of her message. The wind
carried the note like a bank tube from tellee
to teller.
Flailing, flying, it went whipping out the window,
winding alongside faster than this speeding
locomotive.
In a matter of seconds, I could barely remember
anything the note said. I wondered what
advice the last few words would have given...
When the time is right I will remember; it will
come back to me. I've got my compass, I'll
find my way.

Traveling Gift: Gently massage these words in your heart often: "I've been guided along the way from the start. I'm equipped with all I need for this journey. I'll figure it out as I go, it's who I am."

Traveling Tip: When we learn to trust ourselves, our instincts will feel more like a compass than just a hunch.

Back Roads, Crummy Roads and Crossroads

I like to drive on gravel roads, or as my friend's daughter calls them: "the old crummy roads." On these old crummy roads I drive slower, think more clearly, and I don't have to watch out for as many vehicles as I do in the wild life. As I drove down my usual crummy road route one day, I saw a duck walk right out in the middle of the road. I slowed down because she appeared to be traveling with intention, and wasn't aware yielding to the car would be in her best interest. I wanted to see if she was a dumb duck or a brave duck. It turned out she was a sage, and I sat back and watched her teach a lesson.

She first walked across the road, and then went back to the ditch she came out of and led a small line of ducklings across. Walking beside them, she then went back, and came out one more time, this time following behind.

They had confidence in their mother's courage, took comfort in her care, and blindly followed her anywhere.

I witnessed on this crummy road a motherduckling miracle. It is how I believe God leads: He walks before us, He walks beside us, and He walks behind us.

Confident in every environment I find myself in because He's there with me; comforted in facing people, places and things I never have because He's already gone there ahead of me, and He always has my back.

My Friend Loneliness

Despite the fact I've experienced His presence, I know every journey, whether crummy road, crossroads, or dessert roads all feel lonely at times.

Loneliness is the uninvited guest guaranteed to show at everyone's party. We may not like him there, but he's coming.

I had often turned to addictions, thinking I was feeding a habit, when I was just trying to distract myself and feed the empty pit of loneliness.

I would stay in or pursue relationships I didn't really want or need and were in neither party's best interest, just trying to ward off loneliness.

I would go places I knew I shouldn't only because I thought I would rather be there than lonely.

I would watch stuff on TV or the Internet that was garbage; not wanting to go to bed because lying in bed would feel so lonely. There was nothing fulfilling in the flashing colors. It wasn't fulfilling, but it was distracting. Entertainment is sometimes just entertainment, other times entertainment is an attempt to distract from how lonely I am.

I've witnessed the busyness approach to not feeling lonely, participated in trying to text my way out of it. But I have found the only way to grow through loneliness is to stop running from it–admit I'm lonely, sit still in it and return to the Source.

When You Feel Alone

When you feel alone, don't settle; settle in Him.
When you desire company, don't compromise.
Don't perform hoping to be chosen, or change
    hoping to be accepted.
Choose to be who you are and accept yourself.
Trust the process and the One who creates.
When you tire of being alone, and feel the only
    way of relief is to pull everything down
    around you, remember you are never alone.
Instead, pray.
Pray for rain.
Wait for rain.
Do a rain dance; it will rain again… It will.

Traveling Gift: Addictions, Temptations and Evil swarm like
flies and buzz like buzzards when loneliness sets in… Pray.

A Prayer for Rain

Father, pour out Fresh Living Water.
Creator, cover me.
Wash over me with it. Take over me with the
    same fresh water that rinses pieces of peace
    rocks at the bottom of a stream.
Completely awake, awakened from a dry dream.
Move in, clouds, to push in a day without thirst, a
    day without hurts, bringing cooling soothing
    soft water.
A day when all dryness is quenched, my soul
    completely drenched.
Warm healing water.
Dry calloused crops crack.
My soul arches its back.
Reaching for you.
I need you.
Don't allow these locusts to have their way with
    me.
Stay with me.
Rushing water filled with power sliding through
    my veins not a single lonely second lived in
    vain 'cause I knew the weather vane would
    come through again.
I will never trust a pessimistic weatherman again.
Allow me to tap into an endless tap, fresh water
    filling every gap.
Pour over me; pour me some of that Fresh Living
    Water… it always rains again.

Dead Stock

On my daughter's eighth birthday she opened a kaleidoscope. They are usually cool for at least two to three minutes and then take their place in the land of forgotten toys. This kaleidoscope, some twenty years old, interested me not because of what it did, but because of the certificate it came with. This kaleidoscope was authentic dead stock. Dead stock is merchandise that was never sold or used, and is often warehoused. I went online and saw all sorts of things still in the box or still with tags on them, never worn, never used, never even tried out. How many of us are holding dead stock? God given gifts warehoused, stored, and collecting dust. Some of them we know about and put away for whatever reason, and plenty of us have unused, untapped and unexplored greatness in us.

I was sitting with Jeremy Brown from Throne Publishing Group talking about people and their personal gifts. Jeremy said he noticed most people don't realize their gifts are special because they have carried them around with them their entire life, so they don't appear that unique since we've grown used to them. I agree with those words. I also think because of what society highlights as "amazing", we don't see the special thing only we carry as being special.

What an incredible responsibility each individual has, to explore and try out everything in us, because there will never be another us. *Commander of the Trunk* is a desperation plea on behalf of your being, a doorbell pounding by the fist of your soul saying… IT IS TIME!

Commander of the Trunk

Self-imposed sanctions, and Civil War scores of
    unheard-of music.
Too many songs have gone unsung.
Too many feet have screamed from the edge of
    the floor, "I wanna dance, I just don't know
    how."
Too many plays that never climbed onto the
    stage.
Too many stories that never crawled across the
    page.
Lives that never got to taste brave.
Taste-bud-chained slaves, never set free, always
    set on crave.
Cleats that never dug deep, slid into third, or
    kicked home.
Dresses never worn, because they were never
    sewn.
Seemingly meaningless seamstresses, all dreams
    hang by a thread.
Basically bank robbers of this world, all thieves
    hang by their head.
Is there any difference between constantly
    hanging your head, and permanently hanging

by it?

Corporate crimes are measured in mere paper
dollars, and noose-tied neckties.

Disregard for dreams, fill mass graves of paper
dolls, and wasted lives.

Seedling dream seeds that never saw a dirt
home…never given rain, never grown.

Listen to the empty, irritable earth-stomach,
know something is missing; hear her hunger
groans.

Procrastination tore down the life-giving
irrigation.

Fear demons were busy cleaning out hearts, on
the attack, leaving chest pains and no chance
for rains.

Driven by doubt, grabbing hold, relentlessly
steering the reins.

Watch your dreams' stagecoach dive over the
orange clay cliff, end-over-end to the bottom.

There are no explosions when stagecoaches
crash; just tangled dusty limbs, gnarly horse
grins, lots of airborne teeth, clumps of hair,
and shame-stained carpet-covered luggage
strewn everywhere.

There is a lot less action when a dream just sits in
its unopened trunk, not a single sticker on it.

It's way too clean to be a real dream.

You gotta bust 'em up in order to bust 'em out.

Never hand the keys of your dreams to society,
First Name: Laughed At, Last name: Doubt.

You are the Commander in Chief of your own
dream guard guardians.

This position cannot be hired out; it's you that
has to fight-protect and nurture these delicate
dreams.

Protect your dreams until they become strong

enough, and then unleash them on this world.
If and when it gets banged up, beat up, and spit
at-lift it up, build it up, and send it out to the
frontlines again.
Living your dreams is a lot like being a parent,
and just as important.
If you are not the living example of commanding
your own dreams, who will show others…
who will show your own children how it's
done?
What dreams do you have sitting in your trunk,
commander?
And if not you, then who will let them out?

Traveling Reflection: What dormant gift in you has been sleeping? What personal potential treasures have been stored up in the trunk? Let's take it out, shake it off, and see what you're working with! No time for fear and second-guessing, let this be fun, and who knows what else it will unlock.

Imperfect Art

"Art is imperfect, stop trying to make it perfect and let it be finished so it can be art, only God is perfect. If we try and remove all the imperfections from art it will no longer be art, same is true for us."

-Dr. Wong

Those were the words shared with me by the acupuncturist as he prepared to impale me with peace. They were much needed words, as I had this inability to let a book I had been working on be finished. I kept finding things I didn't feel where "good enough". As I was struggling with this, I was also not feeling up to par as a father, or as a human being in general. Trying to make things perfect is the worst recipe for peace. Sometimes out of admitting and accepting our shortcomings we not only become human, but we can be the art we were intended to be.

I wrote a note to my daughter on one of those
nights I felt I hadn't done anything right in a while.
She said I could share with you these words that
started in my heart and grew into this card:

For All the Times

For all the things I didn't know how to teach, you
    deserve to know them, so go and learn them.
For all the things I couldn't afford to give you,
    you are worth it. If you still want them, go
    and earn them.
For all the questions left unanswered.
If you feel the need, the need to know, go, go find
    your answers.
For all the things I didn't know how to give you,
    you deserve them, so go, go get them.
My love, my logic, my methods. All imperfect.
    Many times looking back in the rearview, way
    too far below par.
Anything left undone, anything you needed to
    hear or have, but never received–this is a note
    for you to know.
It was never from a lack of love for you, or a lack
    of trying.

You are worth every penny ever spent, everything
faced, Heaven or Hell sent.
If you see it, and you hear "go get it," go get it
then.
Take whatever it is you feel you need, and leave
the rest.
For all the times I spoke too quick.
For all the times I spoke too loud.
For the times when you needed me to speak up,
but I didn't.
For the times when you didn't need me to say
anything, but I did.
I pray God will pull the weeds of those words
from your mind; He would wipe any traces of
those times left in your heart.
Please just know I always love you for who you
are, wherever you are, the way you are.
Please know that.
Hold onto whatever makes you feel loved, and
leave the rest.
Disregard all the other things I have ever said or
done.
They are not important.
You are.

Traveling Gift: We do our best and we will still blow it.
Give and give and still feel like we should have said, done, given
more–been there more, or maybe been there as a better version of
ourselves.

Admitting to people we screwed up and didn't always live our
lives perfectly gives them the permission to do the same; it also lets
them know that in our imperfections we still love them and their
imperfections.

Bulldog Wisdom

While I write from the kitchen table I like little noise and few distractions. Our bulldog Ginger lies under the kitchen table. In a few words she is: meat, fur, fart, and chainsaw style snoring. It's an interesting relationship. This past year she started carrying her hind leg, which led to the discovery that she needed hip surgery. After surgery and a month of healing, the veterinarian told me during the checkup she shouldn't still be carrying her hind leg. He told me if she wasn't walking on it again in a week she should see a pet physical therapist.

I wasn't willing to pay for the therapist, but I was willing to put the time in to break her of a habit she formed. I took it as part of my writing break every day to take the bulldog out and teach her the leg still works. She fought it every day. She stared at me from atop the deck with eyes that said, "well, pick me up and carry me down like you have been." Like most habits, hers had started to involve other people. The stare downs and habit breaking took weeks, and some days she would refuse the progress she had made. The key to removing bad habits: once removed never return to them.

In the beginning the bulldog needed to limp; it alleviated her pain. Once it was fixed the limp no longer served her well. If she continued to limp she would eventually damage the other hip.

This is how most habits form. It's not intentional: we all develop habits out of circumstances and environments we are unaware of. The old habits may have served us by numbing pain or enduring painful environments, situations and people. Destructive habits often start out as distractions to sooth from the pain. In the beginning they do the job. Later on the pain they cause outweighs the payoff they used to promise.

My friend Denny always advised me to work on removing the habit that, in his words: "was going to kill my ass first." If you have habits in your life you know are not good for you, go after the most destructive one first; don't be distracted by taking them all on. If you have a drinking problem and weight to lose, forget about the weight and get rid of the drinking. You will get to the weight in time, but never get around to it if you're dead.

The gift of 5 minutes
We can do anything for five minutes. Do whatever it is you need to do for five minutes and build on that. Use the power of five minutes to stop or start anything–to eat something healthy you'd rather not put in your mouth, or to stop eating something we no longer wish to put in our body. Use five minutes to sit still. Breathe for five, walk for five, or find the courage to talk for five. Use five minute magic to do whatever it is you feel you were unable to do. And when we feel like we got nothing in us to face whatever we're facing, remember you got five minutes in you. You can use the momentum of 5 minutes to reshape habits.

A hero is no braver than an ordinary man, but he is braver five minutes longer.

-Ralph Waldo Emerson

Traveling Reflection: List the habits you know hold you back. One by one, like weeding a garden, remove them from your path. Once you've put in the work, remember they cannot come to your rescue anymore. The habit will call from the past and plea for "one more time!" Don't go back, yes it's a trap!

Traveling Heads Up

Habits are powerful, habits are difficult, and habits are not creative. By not creative I mean they all push their power on us in similar ways. If you look at a habit, like a man walking down the street, and you decide to start choking the man, he will fight you for his life. The habit is alive in you; you are basically taking its life by taking it out, so it will naturally fight us. There will be a struggle. Use their patterns in your favor. Habits are not creative because they use similar, clever, but consistently similar lines on everyone. Much like people who are the controllers in an abusive relationship, the habits will play subtle phrases in our mind like: "Who do you think you are without me?" "You're nothing without me, boring without me, will have nothing to do without me?" "People won't like you without me; you won't enjoy life without me." "You're not strong enough to leave me, you will always struggle with staying away." Here is truth: We already know the kind of person we've become with these habits, and have realized for whatever reason it is no longer working. Be encouraged and focus on the winds of change that will reveal the new unexplored pieces of you that can only be brought to the surface by leaving the old habits behind.

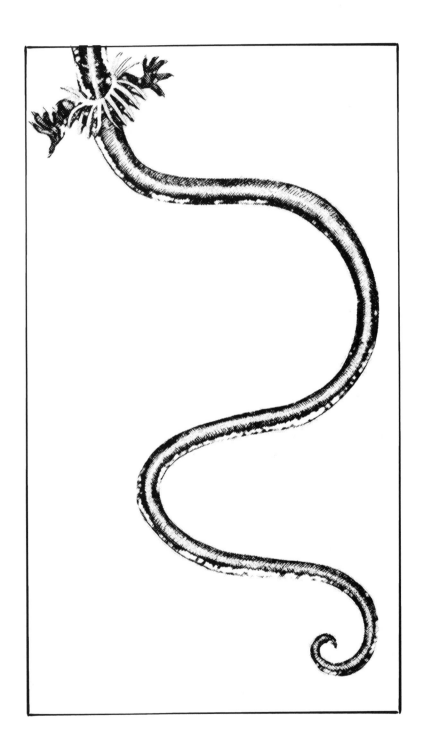

Lizard Wisdom

They were some of the best words I had ever been given.

I was packing my bags for a work trip my daughter wasn't going to be able to come on.

While I packed my bags, she asked why I wasn't bringing my swimsuit. I told her I usually just swim with her, and if she doesn't come with I don't swim.

My words appeared to offend and confuse. With the expression on her face, you would have thought I told her Santa wasn't real.

She said: "*Well swim for me, daddy*"

Those words ring in my ears on a lot of days when there are a lot of things I don't feel like doing.

Swim for me, daddy.

There are plenty of days I have no desire to start what I should be doing, little courage to finish any project, and stop hunting for inspiration. Next to my computer sits a small box filled with notes, pictures, tiny tokens and totems of people—personal motivations to remind we why I really do what I do. Then I can get back to work. I can do this in spite of the distractions, the discouragement, and the procrastination dragon we all face… The Idunwanna Iguana!!

The Idunwanna

The Idunwanna has teeth like a piranha.
The Idunwanna is native to everywhere but the
    Bahamas.

That is, until I get there. Then he shows up in a
    purple print Hawaiian tint skirt and starts
    barking in my ear.
The Idunwanna howls at me like I'm the moon
    and he's… well… he's a fricking Idunnwanna.
You know what they are like; you know the
    things they say. I have a report due in three
    hours
and the Idunwanna would prefer I do anything
    and everything but what is supposed to be
    done first. She encourages me to write a poem
    about her species and their mental mating
    habits.
You know how they breed with every task,
    how they relentlessly gnaw at the head of
    productivity. They shamelessly hump the
    leg of every ladder rung to success, and
    shamelessly lift their leg on deadlines.
The result of this precious pet?

Life starts to look like a jogger who has forgotten
a plastic poo bag, running behind a Great
Dane on a rainy day.
How and where do I start to pick up all this wet
$%t?
If we play fetch with this ungrateful, greedy beast
we saved from the pound, we will always
wind up being the one doing all the chasing.
We become the pet of the pet.
Put the Idunwanna to sleep. It's the only way to
survive. Euthanize the voice that takes your
attention or euthanize your task. It's a choice
between the two every time.
The needle is in your hand. Who takes the needle,
the pet or the project?
Who will win the battle for the next five minutes,
the spiny-faced dream-evaporating demon
of procrastination, or our pursuit of our
purpose? I dunknow, but I know I Idunwanna
another Iguana.

"No more Excuses or procrastination! Stop allowing your days to be stolen by busy nothingness."

-Dr. Steve Maraboli

Traveling Tip: List your motivations. The people we use as motivations don't have to be alive. We don't even have to know them personally. The more motives we have the less likely we are to give up.

Traveling Gift: Inside my wooden motive box are trinkets, tokens, notes, and pictures that motivate me. They motivate me to do my work. They motivate me to take care of myself. They are stronger than the thoughts of "give up. Not today. Hit the snooze one more time." There are phrases and names written on the outside that make me smile and give me courage. There is even a tiny grim reaper figurine inside that likes to encourage me with a smile while I write. It's a house for my recovery coins. It has pictures of people, artwork from orphans, and all sorts of motivational treasures more valuable than gold.

I will place my alarm on the box if I need to wake up extra early, and the box always trumps the snooze button. On days when I feel insecure or unmotivated to write, it's parked right next to my laptop. Just looking at it charges me. I don't even need to open it. Other days sifting through its content gives me exactly what I need to put one foot in front of the other. If it works for you, grab a shoebox, envelope, or something to represent your motives in the life you wish to lead. And visit it often.

Prison Wisdom

I sat with Joe in a deli. We talked about the beauty of his culture, the prison sentence he served, and how he had chosen to change how he was living.

When you eat with someone who's been in prison for a period of time, you'll notice they hold their silverware with a prison style, very similar to military style where the utensil looks more like a scoop on the end of a crane with a methodic shoveling motion.

They also use their arms to section off their food. Forearms staked out like borders entrenched around their meal. We all develop habits out of circumstances and our environments that we are unaware of. You will also notice while spending time with someone who has served time that we are all a series of circumstances and choices away from a prison sentence. We have more similarities than differences. And you will see a powerful piece of the human spirit.

I wanted to meet with Joe because I noticed something in my interactions with him, and watching him interact with others that intrigued me.

I have met so many people over the years that, once in prison, seem unable to stay out. But Joe had not only stayed out, he was thriving on the outside. I had one question for Joe: "Why do you believe your story is different?"

First Joe told me about a man from a church who visited him on a regular basis while he was in prison. He treated Joe like a son (both of Joe's parents passed away while he was in prison).

There was also a group that had a metal working company in the prison, and they not only gave Joe a job while he was in prison, but they made him a manager of one of their operations after he was released. Joe found people who loved him, and Joe found purpose in doing something he loved.

Joe said he noticed most people put stumbling blocks in their own path. Most people place the same mistakes over and over, in their own way, by their own doing. "Life is hard enough; I don't need to keep tripping over my same problems. I have to clear my path of the things I put there."

Another thing I noticed at church was, a lot of times, people were trying to help ex-inmates adjust to the outside. Joe seemed to be the one helping people adjust. Joe told me this started when he was in prison. He felt people caring for him, and felt the need to care for others.

Everything Joe said made sense, and holds true for someone inside or outside of prison walls. The key ingredient here is the act of full circle living.

In order for people to stay sober, stay out of prison, or for anyone to stay on a path of the highest versions of themselves, they must turn around and find someone else on the path and help them on their journey.

When we help people in a way that is healthy for both of us, we fill a part of the soul that cannot be filled by anything else. It puts a charge in you. It fills you with wisdom, courage, and love the way nothing else can.

When I sit with people, in a prison, orphanage, or recovery center I give them something for their stories and their souls to ricochet off of. What they give me, I can't explain it, but when you've found the group that fills your soul, you'll know.

Traveling Gift: Find the group that completes the circle of your journey by spending time with them, and helping them in a way that is healthy for both of you. I keep a checklist of things I need to survive; it's like an action survival kit. I look at my calendar to see when was the last time I spent time with one of these groups of people on my list. It's interesting how my level of personal peace often depends on this list being fulfilled.

Traveling Tip: No matter how much we accomplish, how much we can bench, or how many activities we busy ourselves with, there will always be a space in our journey which can only be filled when we fulfill serving a certain group of people. Find yours. Do it often. You'll love it.

"*The meaning of life is to find your gift. The purpose of life is to give the gift away.*"

-Pablo Picasso

Butterflies and Razor Wire

I waited for my clearance escort to arrive on the
    south end of the north annex prison building.
I looked down at the pounded pavement cracks
    in the concrete under my feet.
I notice the same materials used for keeping men
    and women in…was currently keeping me out.
I notice a butterfly effortlessly pass back and forth
    over the walls I waited to enter. On the other
    side of these same walls souls hoped for an exit.
I entered temporarily through the eyes of the
    butterfly; she was freer than any of us could
    ever pray to be.
I watched this butterfly fly over through and
    around the razor wire, her soft velvet wings
    glide by metal barbs.
She passed restless souls listening to the ticks of
    time–theirs, and mine.
I am going inside, and spending time with those,
    serving time, will set a piece of me free.
I am going inside, and by giving them a piece of
    my time; I will set a piece of them free.
Two pieces together making a whole–filling a
    hole full of peace and freedom.

EVERYTHING I CHOOSE
TO CARRY HAS WEIGHT...
EVERYTHING.

Travel Light

At the cash register I often receive a mandatory sales pitch from store clerks for some sort of additional plastic card that comes with amazing promises of vast riches, and glorious adventure to their store. I decline 100% of the time. When they try the second pre-packaged sales pitch line, my response is always the same: "No thank you, I like to travel light." In return, I often get a cross between a grin, slightly amused and somewhat confused. It's truth. I don't even want to carry a sliver of anything in my wallet. Because everything I carry, no matter what it is, everything–including those cards–all carry some sort of weight.

This world's responsibility weight scale tends to get extremely off-balance, with some people taking no responsibility for themselves, and others believing they are responsible for more than their share. Somewhere in the middle we can find a healthy balance.

I have an eighty-pound dumbbell in my garage to remind me of the physical weight I used to carry on my body. It is a reminder I no longer wish to carry it anymore.

I was trying to use the eighty-pound weight as an example one morning when I saw my daughter mentally trying to carry someone else's responsibility.

I could see the worry on her face and couldn't imagine what it was doing inside her body.

I said, "Anita, do you think you could carry that 80lb dumbbell in the garage around with you today?" One of many reasons why I love her: without hesitation or doubt, her response was: "Yeah." I asked her if she thought it would be hard to do other stuff during her day while she carried it. I explained how even though I'm older and have figured out ways to maneuver and manage weight over the years, there is no way I can live my day the way I'm supposed to lugging that extra weight around. She's smart. She didn't need an explanation. She knew exactly what I was talking about. And even while I was trying to coach her out of mentally carrying the load of someone else, I had to be careful I wasn't doing the same thing and trying to carry hers, because I wanted to. Out of love we often try and relieve others of the weight they bear, but it's not reality.

Here's reality: I cannot absorb anyone's pain for them; I cannot carry any weight in their personal universe for them. We can care for them. We cannot carry for them.

Helping people is part of our life equation. Trying to carry their pain, physically, or mentally is not. Some people try it physically by "doing, doing, doing" for everyone. Not your job. Some people mentally suffer by replaying the pains or problems of others over and over again in their own mind. If I find myself doing this, I remind myself that my mental suffering for someone else's suffering does nothing to alleviate their situation. I must choose to funnel and focus those thoughts into something positive for them or someone else.

Traveling Tip: This is the balance side to the previous chapter. Stay on your side of the scale, allow others the gift of hauling their own weight. We can offer encouragement and love instead of false hope and unrealistic promises. This reality-based way of living also allows us the strength we need to carry our own weights and travel light.

"If you try to pick up pain of someone else that they should be carrying themselves you're going to get beaten up."

> -Robert Bly, Interview into the Deep: Male Mysteries

Take time to work, it is the price of
   success.
Take time to think, it is the source of
   power.
Take time to play, it is the secret of
   perpetual youth.
Take time to read, it is the foundation
   of wisdom.
Take time to be friendly, it is the road
   to happiness.
Take time to love, and be loved, it is the
   privilege of the gods.
Take time to share, life is too short to
   be selfish.
Take time to laugh, laughter is the
   music of the soul.

                        —Irish Prayer, Author Unknown

Mascot Wisdom

When my daughter Anita was five years old, she would sell anything she could find to people walking by our house. She skipped
the lemonade stand racket, and peddled dandelions to the women
walking by. And she hustled grasshoppers as pets to the kids they
pushed in strollers. Make no mistake, she was not out there to have
someone pat her on the head and say, "well aren't you precious!" She
was out there to do business. When people patronized her with their
compliments, she refused to be written off as a cute sideshow. She
only stepped up her sales pitch. I often sat on my porch reading and
smiling as I heard her say things like: "If you buy something from
me I will let your kids throw a handful of Snaps." "If you don't have
cash you can come back and I'll save it for you, or I also take credit
cards." The Snaps firecrackers I knew she had saved from the fourth
of July, but I wasn't sure about the credit card machine. Some days
she would dress herself in costumes to get the attention of people
going by, and after a while I noticed she started dressing up the
neighborhood kids in costumes so she could focus on the selling.

   She saved her money and at the age of nine started her own
mascot business. The company has two mascots in the stable, Dexter
the Dragon and David the Tiger. She has done multiple appearances
with the mascots, and after a cancer fundraiser for kids I asked her
why she liked being a mascot so much. I always thought it was about

performing, but her words showed me it was a space in this world in which she didn't feel like she had to perform at all. Her reason below for why she loves being a mascot, to me, is what love should look and feel like.

"People love you as soon as you show up. They don't know you, or know anything about you. And they love you and love that you're there, that's it. People just love you for no reasons."
　　　　　　　　　　　-Anita Elizabeth Jacobs, very wise business woman

Traveling Truth: When held, received, and given, there is nothing more powerful than love. At times we will need every ounce of courage we have not to close off from it, give up on it, or withhold it.

Love can stare down fear, burn down obstacles, light the path, reveal a new path, and give us courage to keep walking our highest path.

Traveling Gift: a woman at small group told me: "We will love you until you learn to love yourself." I thought it was interesting because I hadn't said anything about not loving myself. The truth was I couldn't even figure out how to like myself at the time.

Let the Dog Out

I first met Denny over nine years ago in his extremely undecorated office. At the time I had no idea God had already chosen this man to save my life. Patiently over the years he would show me how to improve my manner of living. The only way I can possibly attempt to repay my friend Denny is by using what he showed me, and not wasting an ounce of him. During one of our many conversations Denny pointed out how most of us love the underdog story. Denny said: "it's because we can all relate. We can see ourselves in them, not a chance in hell of making it, and not a chance in hell we're giving up either."

Under Dog

I've always liked the underdog.
There is a Helen Keller Type awareness of his
    own circumstance.
It appears as though he is completely unaware
    of how far under he actually is, how little of a
    chance he actually has.
It's like everyone else sees how far gone he is but
    him.
And yet at the same time he is more aware than
    anyone else could ever possibly be.
There is something about the underdog where
    you would be quick to write it off as "luck" or
    "chance," but when you look at him you know
    he has never been introduced to luck, and
    probably never even been in the same room
    as chance.
Watch.
When the underdog shakes loose the collar and
    chain.
Watch.
When the collar of circumstance can no longer
    holds back and keeps strapped the shoulders
    that have carried the weight of too much and

too many for far too long.

Instead of growing too weary to move, they have
become too strong to contain.

Now nothing will ever be the same.

Watch.

When the chain finally snaps.

When the chains of you will never get out of here,
or go anywhere finally snaps.

Watch.

The dog never knew when the steel that stole
would finally give, but he knew it would give
out before he ever did.

Watch.

Stand back and watch, avoid thoughts of "how
did it happen," "how could that possibly be."
Don't try and justify, just...

Watch.

When you see the underdog, you see his
surroundings, his appearance, his past.

He only sees himself, a corner of himself so few
have ever caught a glimpse of. And what they
have seen, they only saw a sliver of a sliver of.
But what they did see, they knew it would be
more than enough.

Just Watch.

When the time aligns and the planets strike
midnight, watch this sleeping beauty pen the
Cinderella story that is no fairy tale.

No one could possibly write about what he is
about to live out.

Watch.

When he pounds the ground, the dust falls...
Everything that was once concrete is no
longer set in stone, and fate streams down his
body, guided between his tightly pulled ribs
like warm muddy water through a canal.

It appears as though the universe has stepped
    aside saying ... "Proceed."
He now controls everything; every outcome is
    now up to him.
Even when he will be done is his own decision.
What you are seeing is something he always
    knew would happen.
The words hopeless, helpless, worthless, loveless,
    will never make sense appearing next to his
    name ever again.
I've always enjoyed a good underdog story.
The next time you see one just
Watch
And for those of you with the dog inside of them,
    I can't wait to see what you are about to do
We will be waiting for you.
We can't wait to watch.

Traveling Gift: Another one of Denny's words of wisdom: "Don't go too far forward, son. You forget where you came from." If you feel like you're currently under a heap of this world, remember you've dug yourself out before and you can do it again. Tap into the inner dog, we all have one.

Traveling Tip: There is a time to surrender and a time to fight, and there is a time to let the dog off the chain.

Weird Wisdom from Witches

I was sitting in a small restaurant with my daughter, and by small I mean the small kind in a small town on a small back alley. A small kind of diner that only takes cash. By small I mean where they use the same dishes from when I ate there in middle school. And now twenty some years later I think I'm staring at the same film on the bottom of the same glass I was drinking out of back then. And I began to wonder which came first, the dishes set or the diner. By small I mean it's hard to tell if it's a diner or an old house or maybe both. You know as well as I do, for whatever reason those are exactly the secret ingredients it takes to make the best cheeseburger, french fries, and chocolate shakes in the universe. My daughter and I both had long days, and we chose to abuse our bodies and massage our taste buds to wind down. While we waited for our food and enjoyed the paintings of a moose, wading in knobby-knee-high electric felt blue water, my daughter said these magical words: "I have a zit on my armpit and it was driving me nuts during my science test." As french fries were being slung and drowned in frosty chocolaty metal malt containers, we discussed how these things happen, how they happen for real!

Science and religion have their theories. Old wives have told their tales. But it is time someone shared truth about where exactly zits come from... witches, man! The craziest, greenest witches you ever never saw are responsible for those things. This malt-stained napkin note led to one of the most revealing truths ever written:

Zit Witch

Zit witch zit witch, it's time for truth, someone
must tell.
This hag of drag and dread lives 2 1/2 miles east
of the edges of hell.
Even the nastiest demons tiptoe the long way
around her hut.
Those who don't... wake up with a zit atop the
bottom of their butt.
She labors over her prized purple-tinted pimple
potions.
Delivered directly by torturous trolls riding on
zit witch cursed traveling moles.
Each night while we rest, foul, fowl zit witch owls
gather their Intel.
Ever hear an owl hoot twice? Hoot... Hoot...
What he's up to is not very nice.
He's relaying the important events we have the
next day.
A date with the man of your dreams?
Tomorrow morning a zit directly on the end of
your nose is where it goes.
Classic zit witch move.
An important job interview?

The troll moves the pimple from the end of your
    nose to just inside it, just enough to drive you
    mad.
The zit witches' only strategy… Deliver Personal
    Pimplistic Tragedy (which is also her mission
    statement printed on her business cards).
Are you preparing for the world's longest science
    test? On the armpit for you!
Who can we call to erase this evil, to hide,
    conceal, squeeze, or remove this mountainous
    mayhem?
No one…
There is no one.
The government isn't big enough.
It's out of Ghostbuster jurisdiction.
The church no longer wants to talk of such things.
We're on our own, folks.
There is only one thing we can do…
Laugh it off.
It really pisses her off.

"Humor was another of the soul's weapons in the fight for self-preservation."

-Viktor E. Frankl

Traveling Gift: Life is heavy–don't forget to breathe, to laugh, and be weird whenever possible on your journey. Keep track of how often you're laughing during the week by yourself, and with your friend and family. We schedule all sorts of things for our health, like exercise, rest, mediation, and many other practices we know we need to make sure are part of our regular routine. A checklist to laugh is no different. I have a weekly lunch with my friend Dan that focuses on pure ridiculousness and laughter. Schedule time to watch your favorite comedians, movies. Or spend time with people you know will offer the healing vibration only laughter can.

Fortune Cookie Wisdom

There are many superstitions on how to eat a fortune cookie. Some say it should be opened before or after the meal. There are different schools of thought on how it should be broken open. Some people put the phrase "in bed" after every fortune they read. My friend Steve eats the cookie unopened swallowing the fortune along with the cookie. My daughter and I grab two cookies each, and if we don't like our fortunes, we trade them.

Sometimes we draw faces on the cookies before we smash them. I have an entire Ziploc bag full of old fortune cookie wisdom I had planned on turning into an art project someday. Or maybe the bag itself is art.

Fortune Cookies

Write on your own slips of paper.

Traveling Courage: Plenty of our days are going to hurt. They are going to suck. We will feel like we've lost more than we've won; we are not going to know what to do or how to possibly face some days, some people, or some situations.

I've learned it is best to wake up every morning and create your own luck.

If the God of this universe decided today was a good day to give me another shot, and if He felt it was worth taking the time, and He chose to fill my lunges up this morning, then it's up to me to figure out what to do with each breathe. And create my own damn luck if I have to.

He gives us the breath, we figure out the next step.

"... most men in a concentration camp believed that the real opportunity of life had past.

Yet, in reality, there was an opportunity and a challenge. One could make a victory of those experiences turning life into an inner triumph, or one could ignore the challenge and simply vegetate, as did the majority of the prisoners. Man's unique opportunity lies in the way he bears his burden. Everything can be taken away from a man but one thing: the last of the human freedoms – to choose one's attitude in any given set of circumstances, to choose one's own way."

-Viktor Frankl

Travel Well

I call my friend Deb because she is wise and honest. She makes incredible homemade desserts, and when I get off track, she lovingly reminds me of who I am. I also call when I know I'm staring at something I wish was someone else's demon or situation to face. I call Deb before taking on a canyon-sized adventure. There has been more than one occasion I needed to hear my favorite piece of advice. She says over the phone in her thick New Jersey accent: "It's going to be fine. It's not going to be easy, but you'll get through on the other side and you know it will be fine. You know from experience it won't be easy, but it will be fine."

"Life is either a daring adventure or nothing at all."

-Helen Keller

Ice

Don't walk so gingerly through life like you are
tiptoeing across ice.
Don't carefully place each step with such
uncertainty.
Slam them down like you control the ground!
The ground can move if that's its wish. But you,
your steps, and the path you lay will not shift.
We will fall, we will fail, and if we didn't, then
what's the point?
Choose to walk where others have walked
around.
Don't fear the steps, or second-guess the ground.
Drown out the fear of failures heckling howling
hounds by listening to the sweet rhythm of
putting one foot in front of the other.
You might not know exactly where you are going,
but make no mistake: you know you are on
your way there.
Travel well, Friend

I'm thankful for the time people have shared with me over the years, and I am thankful they chose to walk different roads, scale tougher terrain, brave paths few choose to walk in order to improve their lives. And I am thankful they chose to then circle around and show me how to find my own path.

For their time, their courage to face their own pain, their graciousness, patience, and the humility to share what they found with fellow travelers. They selflessly lent me some of their courage until I found my own, loved me until I could figure out how to love myself, and never asked for anything in return. My life and this book would remain rough drafts of mostly empty pages without you:

Anita, Isabella, Mom, Dad, Chad and Tessa, Ducky, Darlene and Lyle Bird, Darlene and Donald Jacobs. Franks, buddy thanks for letting me call and say I love writing this book and then the next day call and say I hate writing this book. Denny Montgomery, Debbie Graham, Tobias G, Don Tripp, The Heidelbergers, Julie Williams, Ryan Vanderbush, and Pam Beck. Veronika Ludweg, thanks for the healing, John and Linda Friel for their works and guidance, thank you, Roy Williams, All the Oh My Cupcake Ninjas. Katie Graham and Mary Utzig for the Grammar Hammer people who love grammar would hate me if it weren't for your endless hrs. of editing. Stolp's, Dawson and Fulton McAllister two of my favorite warriors on this planet. Fortune favors the bold MR. Jones thanks for telling me to scratch my own itch. Steve Chase, Geronimo. Steve Dunn and The Onida Town Sisters. Jody Staples for building the website, Hunter B. you're awesome. Daniel Son and the Needy Flies. Kyle Hammer you're like a brother. My friend and an inspiration Nearly Normal George Norman who always walked barefoot and carried his headphones in that purple Crown Royal bag, thanks for telling me I should listen to Ray Charles and find good Jazz tapes. Jerry James, Zoe, you are a great writer, keep putting pen to paper! People I don't know personally but I felt like I did when I read their words: Dan Millman, Melody Beaty, Steven Pressfield, Julia Cameron, Rober Bly, and Anne Lamont. Jeremy Brown for your guidance along the way, Throne Publishing and the Throne Team. The lady at the checkout of the grocery store who looked at my groceries and said: "Travel well today, sir."

About the Author

Travis D. Jacobs is the author of more than 1.5 books; he lives in a tiny fort in South Dakota with his super cool daughter and their trusty English bulldog, who has also chosen to travel well through this universe.

FREE Rhythm Wisdom Videos
www.rhythmwisdom.com

Learn about Rhythm Wisdom Word SMITHIN Workshops
www.rhythmwisdom.com

Book Travis to Speak at your event
www.rhythmwisdom.com